STAY WEIRD

STAY WEIRD

An Hachette UK Company
www.hachette.co.uk

Summersdale Publishers Ltd
Part of Octopus Publishing Group Limited
Carmelite House
50 Victoria Embankment
LONDON
EC4Y 0DZ
UK

www.summersdale.com

Printed and bound in the Czech Republic

ISBN: 978-1-78783-255-8

To............................
From.........................

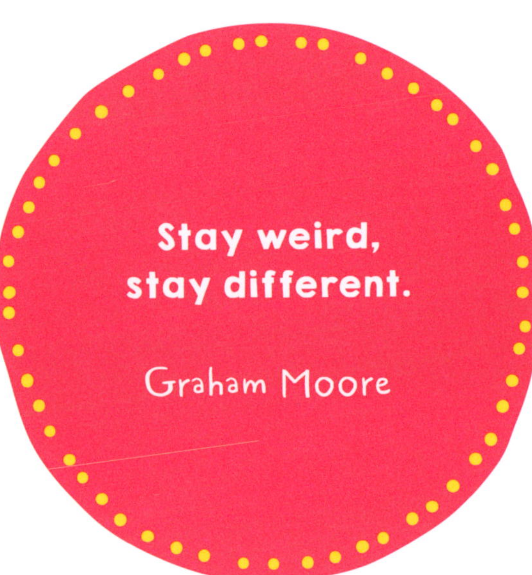
Stay weird,
stay different.
Graham Moore

**Mix a little foolishness
with your serious plans.
It's lovely to be silly
at the right moment.**

Horace

LIFE IS TOO SHORT TO WORRY ABOUT WHAT OTHERS SAY ABOUT YOU.

Why be normal
when you can be

I PROMISE YOU THAT EACH AND EVERY ONE OF YOU IS MADE TO BE WHO YOU ARE.

Selena Gomez

Embrace your weirdness.

Cara Delevingne

The more you praise and celebrate your life, the more there is in life to celebrate.

Oprah Winfrey

WHAT MAKES YOU DIFFERENT MAKES YOU SPECIAL

BELIEVE IN YOUR FLYNESS AND CONQUER YOUR SHYNESS.

You're perfect when you're comfortable being yourself.

Ansel Elgort

YOU ARE MAGNIFICENT BEYOND MEASURE, PERFECT IN YOUR IMPERFECTIONS AND WONDERFULLY MADE.

Abiola Abrams

You're not here
to be average;
you're here to be

Being your true self is the most effective formula for success there is.

Danielle LaPorte

The reward for conformity is that everyone likes you but yourself.

Rita Mae Brown

CHERISH FOREVER WHAT MAKES YOU UNIQUE, 'CAUSE YOU'RE REALLY A YAWN IF IT GOES.

Bette Midler

QUIRKY
IS
COOL

Joseph Campbell

WHY FIT IN WHEN YOU WERE BORN TO STAND OUT?

Every day brings new choices.

Martha Beck

WEIRD IS A SIDE-EFFECT OF BEING AWESOME

SELF-ACCEPTANCE IS MY REFUSAL TO BE IN AN ADVERSARIAL RELATIONSHIP WITH MYSELF.

Nathaniel Branden

Optimism is the faith that leads to achievement. Nothing can be done without hope and confidence.

Helen Keller

ACT THE WAY YOU WANT TO FEEL.

Gretchen Rubin

You're one of
a kind –

The way you carry yourself is influenced by the way you feel inside.

Marilyn Monroe

IT DOESN'T MATTER WHAT YOU DO. IT MATTERS WHO YOU ARE.

I have insecurities of course, but I don't hang out with anyone who points them out to me.

Adele

YOUR IMPERFECTIONS
ARE WHAT MAKE
YOU UNIQUE

WHENEVER YOU FIND YOURSELF ON THE SIDE OF MAJORITY, IT IS TIME TO PAUSE AND REFLECT.

Mark Twain

Most of the shadows of this life are caused by standing in one's own sunshine.

Ralph Waldo Emerson

Embrace the
glorious mess
that you are.

Elizabeth Gilbert

LIFE'S TOO SHORT TO FOLLOW THE CROWD

I am the master
of my fate:
I am the captain
of my soul.

William Ernest Henley

FIND OUT WHO YOU ARE AND DO IT ON PURPOSE.

Be congruent, be authentic, be your true self.

Mahatma Gandhi

DON'T BE AFRAID TO LOOK

SILLY

Be fearless in breaking new boundaries.

Christina Aguilera

In order to be irreplaceable one must always be different.

Coco Chanel

THE OPPOSITE
OF BRAVERY
IS NOT
COWARDICE
BUT
CONFORMITY.

GOOFY AND
PROUD OF IT

TO BE BEAUTIFUL MEANS TO BE YOURSELF. YOU DON'T NEED TO BE ACCEPTED BY OTHERS. YOU NEED TO ACCEPT YOURSELF.

Thích Nhất Hạnh

DO YOUR THING, AND DON'T CARE IF THEY LIKE IT.

Who you are authentically is alright. Who you are is beautiful and amazing.

Laverne Cox

In a world full of
Cheerios, be a

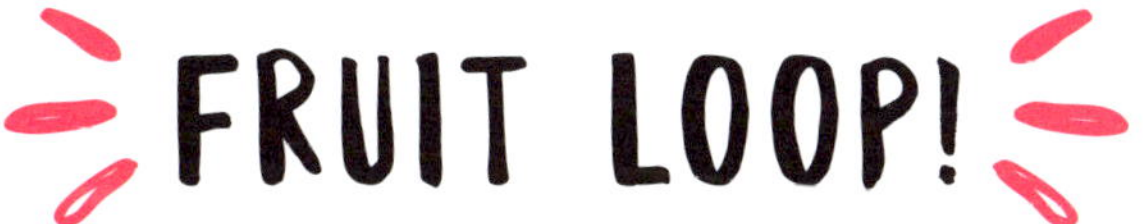

I'M NOT AFRAID OF STORMS, FOR I AM LEARNING HOW TO SAIL MY SHIP.

Louisa May Alcott

If people did not sometimes do silly things, nothing intelligent would ever get done.

Ludwig Wittgenstein

CREATE THE HIGHEST, GRANDEST VISION POSSIBLE FOR YOUR LIFE, BECAUSE YOU BECOME WHAT YOU BELIEVE.

Oprah Winfrey

Being normal is

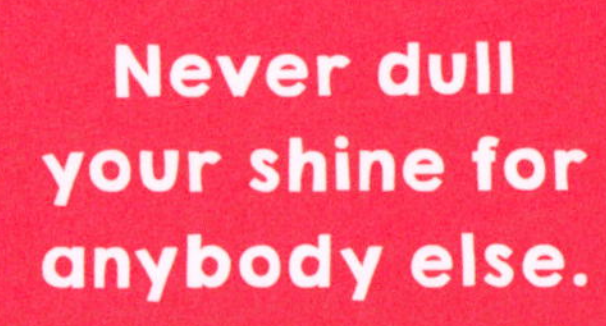

Never dull your shine for anybody else.

Tyra Banks

You don't get harmony when everybody sings the same note.

Anonymous

Embrace who you are. Literally. Hug yourself. Accept who you are.

Ellen DeGeneres

YOU BRING THE COLOUR TO A BLACK AND WHITE WORLD

I'M ONE OF THOSE REGULAR WEIRD PEOPLE.

No one can make you feel inferior without your consent.

Eleanor Roosevelt

JUST DO WHAT WORKS FOR YOU, BECAUSE THERE WILL ALWAYS BE SOMEBODY WHO THINKS DIFFERENTLY.

Michelle Obama

DON'T FEED THE TROLLS

You're always with yourself, so you might as well enjoy the company.

Diane von Furstenberg

OVERCOME THE NOTION THAT WE MUST BE REGULAR... IT ROBS YOU OF THE CHANCE TO BE EXTRAORDINARY.

Uta Hagen

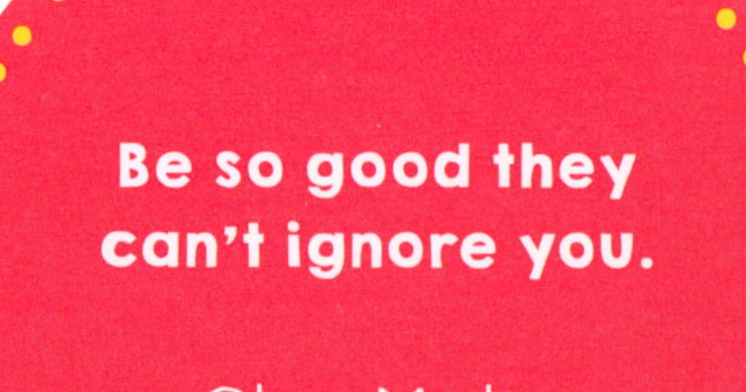

Be so good they can't ignore you.

Steve Martin

IT'S A WONDERFUL DAY TO BE

WEIRD!

It is better to fail in originality than to succeed in imitation.

Herman Melville

People say that you're going the wrong way when it's simply a way of your own.

Angelina Jolie

BEWARE; FOR I AM FEARLESS, AND THEREFORE POWERFUL.

Mary Shelley

ALL YOU
NEED IS YOU

DON'T COMPARE YOURSELF WITH ANYONE IN THIS WORLD. IF YOU DO SO, YOU ARE INSULTING YOURSELF.

Bill Gates

BEING DIFFERENT GIVES THE WORLD COLOUR.

Do you. Wear what you want to wear. Be an individual. Be unique and live your best life.

Kali Uchis

WEIRD IS
BEAUTIFUL

THE THINGS THAT MADE YOU WEIRD AS A KID MAKE YOU GREAT TODAY.

SMILE AND LET EVERYONE KNOW THAT TODAY YOU'RE A LOT STRONGER THAN YOU WERE YESTERDAY.

Drake

You cannot live your life looking at yourself from someone else's point of view.

Penélope Cruz

Be your own
kind of

Confidence is preparation. Everything else is beyond your control.

Richard Kline

Be happy with being you. Love your flaws. Own your quirks. And know that you are just as perfect as anyone else, exactly as you are.

Ariana Grande

TELL ME, WHAT IS
IT YOU PLAN TO DO
WITH YOUR ONE WILD
AND PRECIOUS LIFE?

Mary Oliver

YOUR CONFIDENCE
LIGHTS UP THE ROOM

Turn your face
to the sun and
the shadows fall
behind you.

Maori Proverb

CREATE THE KIND OF SELF THAT YOU WILL BE HAPPY TO LIVE WITH ALL YOUR LIFE.

Golda Meir

One can never consent to creep when one feels an impulse to soar.

Helen Keller

YOU DO

YOU

The difference between ordinary and extraordinary is that little extra.

Jimmy Johnson

Uniqueness is
what makes
you the most
beautiful.

Lea Michele

IT'S NOT YOUR JOB TO LIKE ME – IT'S MINE.

EVERYONE
ZIGS, SO ZAG

Be yourself. Believe in what you know and not what others say about you.

Hailee Steinfeld

EVERY WEIRD
THING ABOUT YOU IS
BEAUTIFUL AND MAKES
LIFE AMAZING.

Kesha

Stay strong and be yourself! It's the best thing you can be.

Cara Delevingne

LET YOUR INNER LIGHT

SHINE!

YOU DON'T NEED ANYBODY TO TELL YOU WHO YOU ARE OR WHAT YOU ARE. YOU ARE WHAT YOU ARE.

John Lennon

Nothing can
dim the light
which shines
from within.

Maya Angelou

MY MOTTO IS: I'M ALIVE, SO THAT MEANS I CAN DO ANYTHING.

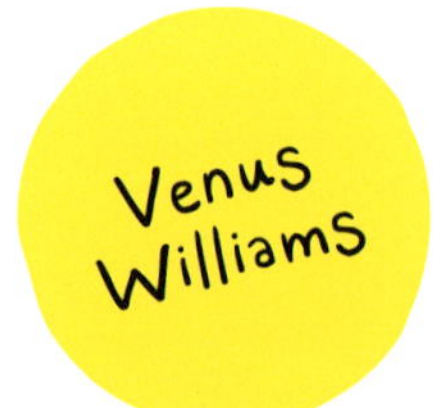

YOU'RE A
LIMITED
EDITION

The formula of happiness and success is just being actually yourself, in the most vivid possible way you can.

Meryl Streep

BELIEVE YOU CAN AND YOU'RE HALFWAY THERE.

Theodore Roosevelt

You laugh at me
because I'm different,
I laugh because
you're all the same.

Jonathan Davis

NEVER LOSE
YOUR SPARKLE

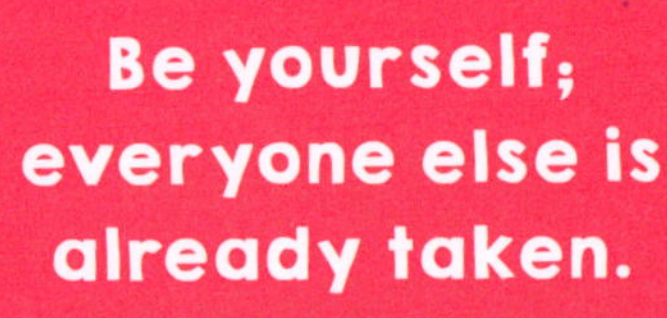

Anonymous

We have to learn
to be our own best
friends because
we fall too easily
into the trap
of being our own
worst enemies.

Roderick Thorp

TO BE YOURSELF IN A WORLD THAT IS CONSTANTLY TRYING TO MAKE YOU SOMETHING ELSE IS THE GREATEST ACCOMPLISHMENT.

Ralph Waldo Emerson

BE FEARLESSLY AUTHENTIC

A good head
and a good heart
are always
a formidable
combination.

Nelson Mandela

I NEVER ALLOW MYSELF TO NOT FEEL CONFIDENT.

The more you are like yourself, the less you are like anyone else, which makes you unique.

Walt Disney

THERE'S NEVER
A DULL MOMENT
WITH YOU

WHEN YOU KNOW YOURSELF YOU ARE EMPOWERED. WHEN YOU ACCEPT YOURSELF YOU ARE INVINCIBLE.

Tina Lifford

Your self-worth is determined by you. You don't have to depend on someone telling you who you are.

Beyoncé

ONE OF THE MOST IMPORTANT THINGS YOU CAN ACCOMPLISH IS JUST BEING YOURSELF.

Dwayne Johnson

YOU ARE AWESOME
JUST AS YOU ARE!

When I have to make decisions, I always choose honesty and I always stay true to myself.

Lizzo

YOUR TIME IS LIMITED, SO DON'T WASTE IT LIVING SOMEONE ELSE'S LIFE.

Steve Jobs

What we do flows from who we are.
Paul Vitale

You are a gem.

WHAT SETS YOU APART CAN SOMETIMES FEEL LIKE A BURDEN AND IT'S NOT. AND A LOT OF THE TIME, IT'S WHAT MAKES YOU GREAT.

Emma Stone

You have to
be unique, and
different, and
shine in your
own way.

Lady Gaga

There's power in looking silly and not caring that you do.

Amy Poehler

LOVE YOURSELF

FiRST

BE YOURSELF. THE WORLD WORSHIPS THE ORIGINAL.

WHEN YOU BECOME THE IMAGE OF YOUR OWN IMAGINATION, IT'S THE MOST POWERFUL THING YOU COULD EVER DO.

RuPaul

I don't get embarrassed easily, and I do silly things all the time!

Emily Osment

LIFE IS MADE FOR LIVING, SO GET OUT THERE!

NORMAL IS NOT SOMETHING TO ASPIRE TO; IT'S SOMETHING TO GET AWAY FROM.

Jodie Foster

Different is good. So don't fit in, don't sit still, don't ever try to be less than what you are.

Angelina Jolie

I finally figured out the only reason to be alive is to enjoy it.

Rita Mae Brown

Believe in

I say if I'm beautiful.
I say if I'm strong.
You will not determine
my story – I will.

Amy Schumer

IT TAKES COURAGE TO GROW UP AND BECOME WHO YOU REALLY ARE.

I DON'T WANT OTHER PEOPLE TO DECIDE WHO I AM. I WANT TO DECIDE THAT FOR MYSELF.

Emma Watson

You're the star of

THE YOU SHOW

JUST WHEN THE
CATERPILLAR THOUGHT
THE WORLD WAS ENDING,
IT BECAME A BUTTERFLY.

Anonymous

What makes
you different
or weird, that's
your strength.

Meryl Streep

The greatest gift you can ever give is your honest self.

Fred Rogers

YOU ARE A
PERFECT RARITY

Be unique.
Be memorable.
Be confident.
Be proud.

Shannon L. Alder

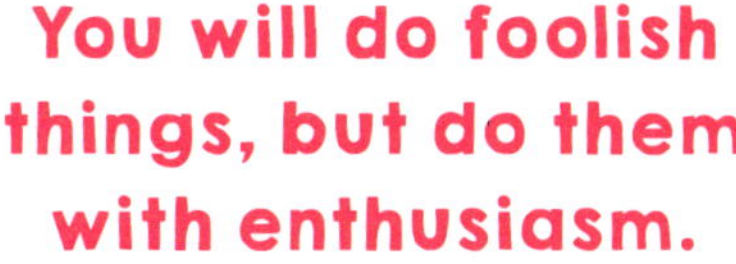

Colette

DOUBT WHOM YOU WILL, BUT NEVER YOURSELF.

WHAT'S "NORMAL" ANYWAY?

Aerodynamically, the bumblebee shouldn't be able to fly, but the bumblebee doesn't know so it goes on flying anyway.

Mary Kay Ash

This above all: to thine own self be true.

William Shakespeare

Love yourself
first and
everything else
falls into line.

Lucille Ball

EMBRACE EVERY FLAW
AND EVERY QUIRK

WHEN I LET GO OF WHAT I AM, I BECOME WHAT I MIGHT BE.

It's weird
not to be weird.

John Lennon

IF YOU'RE PRESENTING YOURSELF WITH CONFIDENCE, YOU CAN PULL OFF PRETTY MUCH ANYTHING.

Katy Perry

NOBODY IS YOU –
THAT IS YOUR
SUPERPOWER

TODAY YOU ARE YOU,
THAT IS TRUER THAN
TRUE. THERE IS NO
ONE ALIVE THAT IS
YOUER THAN YOU.

Dr Seuss

Find out who you are
and be that person...
Find that truth, live that
truth and everything
else will come.

Ellen DeGeneres

WE ALWAYS MAY BE WHAT WE MIGHT HAVE BEEN.

IF YOU CAN ACCEPT YOURSELF, THAT'S ALL YOU NEED

Be silly.
You're allowed to be silly. There's nothing wrong with it.

Jimmy Fallon

Jean Anouilh

If you have an idea, you have to believe in yourself when no one else will.

Sarah Michelle Gellar

BE A VOICE,
NOT AN ECHO

THERE'S A WHOLE CATEGORY OF PEOPLE WHO MISS OUT BY NOT ALLOWING THEMSELVES TO BE WEIRD ENOUGH.

Alain de Botton

I do not belong
to anyone but
myself and
neither do you.

Ariana Grande

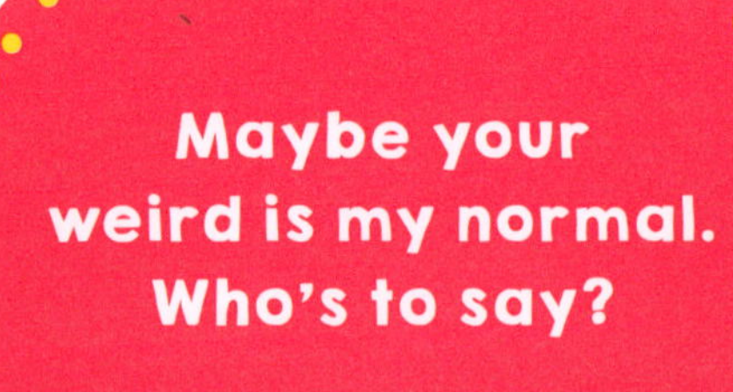
Maybe your
weird is my normal.
Who's to say?
Nicki Minaj

STAY

WEIRD

If you're interested in finding out more about our books, find us on Facebook at **Summersdale Publishers** and follow us on Twitter at **@Summersdale**.

www.summersdale.com

IMAGE CREDITS

Endpapers © Mint and Chips/Shutterstock.com

Sprinkles – pp.9, 13, 17, 28, 34, 36, 40, 53, 57, 64, 76, 80, 85, 93, 101, 104, 117, 122, 136, 142, 145, 154, 157 © Mint and Chips/Shutterstock.com

Black and yellow pattern – pp.10, 22, 30, 38, 49, 60, 70, 82, 90, 98, 109, 125, 149 © theromb/Shutterstock.com

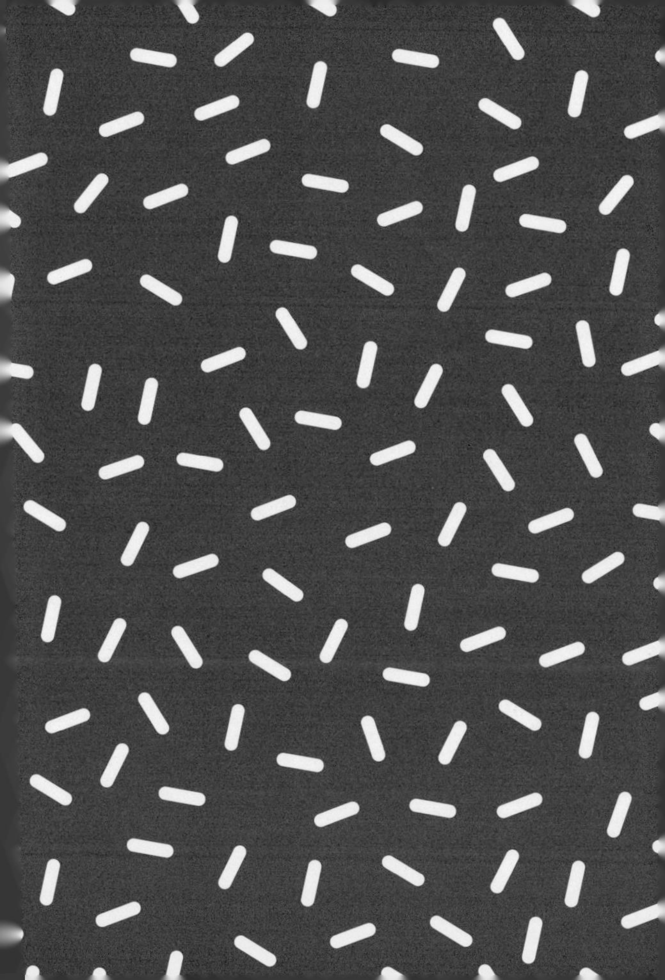